Christian Lehnert

Wickerwork

Translated from the German
by Richard Sieburth

archipelago books

First published in German as *Cherubinischer Staub. Gedichte*
and *Opus 8. Im Flechtwerk* by Suhrkamp Verlag

First Archipelago Books Edition, 2025

Library of Congress Cataloging-in-Publication Data
available upon request.

ISBN 9781962770248

The authorized representative in the EU for product safety and
compliance is eucomply OÜ, Pärnu mnt 139b-14, 11317 Tallinn, Estonia,
hello@eucompliancepartner.com, +33 757690241

Archipelago Books
232 3rd Street #A111
Brooklyn, NY 11215
www.archipelagobooks.org

Distributed by Penguin Random House
www.penguinrandomhouse.com

This work is made possible by the New York State Council on the Arts with
the support of the Office of the Governor and the New York State Legislature.
Funding for the publication of this book was provided by a grant from the Carl
Lesnor Family Foundation and the Hawthornden Foundation. We are grateful to
the Goethe-Institut for providing translation support for this title.

PRINTED IN CANADA

CONTENTS

Listening In

"Thus the first line is named:
the sound you make, listening in."

B ORN IN DRESDEN IN 1969, Christian Lehnert grew up under the grey godless skies of the German Democratic Republic, eventually discovering his own adolescent path to dissidence in the illuminations of modern poetry (Rilke, Trakl, Bobrowski) and the mysteries of Christian faith. When called up for obligatory military service at age eighteen, he was, as a confirmed member of the Evangelical Lutheran church, granted conscientious objector status for his refusal to bear arms, only to be conscripted as a Bausoldat (or construction soldier) into a platoon of fellow slave laborers engaged in the hellhole excavation of secret military installations and contaminated chemical waste sites. Upon the fall of the Wall in 1989 (known to Germans as *Die Wende*, or The Turn), Lehnert was released from the army, now free to pursue advanced degrees in theology in Leipzig and Berlin, during the course of which he spent a year in Jerusalem at the Benedictine Abbey of the Dormition on Mount Zion to follow an ecumenical curriculum grounded in Old Testament, Eastern Orthodox, and Judaic studies, in addition to instruction in Arabic—a classic journey to the Holy Land in search of origins, with its Biblical wastes and scorched desert monasteries taking pride of place in his early poems.

After his sojourn in the East, Lehnert's spiritual *Wende* took him to Santiago de Compostela, where he spent two years training his eye in the mannerist enigmas of Spanish baroque painting while exploring the wild Galician landscapes of Finisterre—the westernmost point of Europe. In 2002, his pilgrimage years over, he returned to his homeland in the former GDR to devote himself to pastoral duties as a Lutheran minister in a small rural community in Saxony southeast of Dresden. Eight years later, he was finally appointed to university positions in the theological faculties of Wittenberg and Leipzig, where he continues to teach today, publishing both poetry and four well-received volumes of essays devoted to such topics as the history of angels, the poetics of Christian liturgy, Paul's first Letter to the Corinthians and the Apocalypse of John—all composed in an idiosyncratic idiom of (negative) theology, rooted in the German Protestant tradition of inner-light mysticism yet conversant with such post-Heideggerian continental philosophers as Levinas, Derrida, Agamben, and Nancy.

This selection of Lehnert's nature poetry, the first to appear in English, has been gathered from his most recent volumes of verse: in receding order, *Opus 8*, *Im Flechtwerk* (*Opus 8*, *Wickerwork*, 2022), *Cherubinischer Staub* (*Cherub Dust*, 2018), and *Windzüge* (*Windstrokes*, 2015). As its title indicates, *Opus 8* signals his eighth book of poetry, while also suggestive of the cataloging of a composer's work. Lehnert's verse is steeped in music, ranging from his refashionings of the hymns of the baroque poet Paul Gerhardt to his libretti for the well-known avant-garde composer Hans Werner Henze. *Opus 8* he describes as having the musical structure of a Bach cantata or fugue, organized along mathematical lines. The book is divided into seven linked chapters or movements, each of which is preceded by epigraphs drawn from the wisdom literature of Meister Eckhart, Jakob Böhme, and the Zohar. These seven sections are in turn each composed of seven contrapuntal poems that face each other across the page: to the left, the solo voicings of a couplet, to the right the chorale of an octave, the former metered as an alexandrine, the latter often as a tetrameter. In the felicitous arithmosophy of this opus, then, 7 x 7 = 49 doublets, adding up to a book-length cycle of 98 poems in all. For reasons of space, I have only included eighteen of these paired poems, typographically laid out with the English above and the German (in grey) below, the texts thus facing upwards downwards, the echo of translation rising from the depths of the original.

The remainder of my selection from *Opus 8* is made up of twenty-eight rhymed couplets, here isolated from their facing octaves as freestanding poems. Such elliptical two-liners (*Zweizeiler* or distichs in German) constitute one of Lehnert's signature verse forms, exemplifying Pound's bilingual dictum that Dichtung = CONDENSARE. Indeed, Lehnert cites the latter's "In A Station of the Metro" as an important impetus for his handling of haiku-like epiphanies. Here is Pound's celebrated poem in its original 1913 ideogrammic printing:

> *The apparition   of these faces   in a crowd :*
> *Petals   on a wet, black   bough .*

However ghostly the sudden surfacing of these visages out of the subterranean Hades of an anonymous modern Metro crowd might be, we are nonetheless here solidly in the realm of what Pound calls *phanopoeia* — "a casting of images on the visual imagination." Compare a typical Lehnert distich:

> *Das Rieseln / dies Gesumm   aus einer mürben Welt /*
> *So lauscht der alter Baum   dem Anlaut / der ihn fällt.*

> *This trickle / this dim hum / of a world / in decay /*
> *An old tree / listens for / what's rotting it away.*

A baroque memento mori of sorts—whose domain is less visual than acousmatic (i.e. involving a sound that is heard without seeing its source, here expressed by the German verb *lauschen*, "to listen to" or "listen for" or "listen in"). Pound is drawn to the outside world, Lehnert to its insides—in this case, those of an ailing tree overhearing the premonitory sound (or *Anlaut*) of the tinder fungus that will eventually take its life. But however different their sensibilities, Lehnert nonetheless follows Pound in deploying what the Japanese call *Ma* (or negative space) to open up intervals within the closed fold of rhyme, each of his virgules indicating a pause of breath or sense, and with the median caesura after the six-syllable hemistich of the German alexandrine marked by a blank musical rest (rendered in my English, to avoid metrical confusion, by another slash mark).

Lehnert's recourse to virgules points back to the typographies of German baroque verse, where the separatrix was often inserted by such poets as Andreas Gryphius as a guide to oral reading. Similarly, Lehnert's predilection for distichs derives not from the classical tradition of the epigram, but rather from the rhymed syllabo-tonic alexandrines that migrated into German prosody in the early seventeenth century via Dutch translations from the French. By the time of the late Renaissance, the term epigram had come to embrace any number of shorter strophic forms, ranging from the couplet through the octaves and tercets of the sonnet, but when it comes to capturing the gist and pith of the baroque *Reimspruch*, Lehnert prefers the taut interwovenness of the rhymed distich—which in his subtitle to *Opus 8* he refers to as *Flechtwerk*, or in its standard English translation, *Wickerwork*, the name I have chosen to give to this volume as a whole.

To delve into the etymology of *Flechtwerk* is to engage in the linguistic equivalent of string theory. The German verb *flechten* reaches back to the Indo-European root **plek* ("to pleat"), which provides the fiber of the Old English "flax," while also giving rise in Latin to the verb *plicare* ("to fold"), which in turn yields the word *simplex* (or "once folded") from which the term "simple" derives—with its opposite, "complex" (or "braided together"), analogously formed from the Latin past participle *plexus*. The further plies of *plicare* include: implicit, explicit, complicit, explicate, implicate, duplicate, replicate, etc. Inspired by the quirky logic of this etymology, theoretical physicist Murray Gell-Mann (discoverer of the Joycean quark) invented the research field he called Plectics to describe the study of the interfoldings of simplicity and complexity within the material universe. Lehnert's *Wickerwork*—the English word comes from the Swedish *vika*, "to bend"—explores a similar (if more Leibnizian: see Deleuze's *Le pli*) plectic universe, its texture articulated by the weave of his strands of distichs, their every prosodic weft and warp looped through the crease of rhyme.

The term *Flechtwerk* invites a number of further etymological ravelings as well, for the word also names the wattle-and-daub facade work of traditional German village architecture (*Im Flechtwerk* thus becoming a metonym for historic in-dwelling), while the verb *flechten* in turn gives rise to the organism known as *Flechte*, or lichen, so called in German because of the way its fungal filaments are braided into a mesh that surrounds its algal cells in an interstitial intimacy of mutually beneficial symbiosis. Among the oldest living organisms on earth, lichen reproduces asexually by dispatching complete monads of itself (Leibnitz again) as it spreads, surviving as a self-sufficient ecological system that in its difference from itself (fungi v. protists) remains ever identical, ever (as Hopkins might put it) "selved." As a long-standing student of Paracelsus's *Herbarius*, Lehnert is alert to the medicinal properties of *Cetraria islandica*, the lichen commonly known as Icelandic moss, but in the following epigram he specifically links its capacity to speak in tongues—lichen comes from the Greek *lichein*, or "to lick"—to the gentle glossolalia of nature:

> *Its tongues lie soft / along gravel and growth ring.*
> *Thus lichen flows / willing to want nothing.*

To flow like lichen spores, not caring when or where, to exist beyond will or want or articulate language—this is that Zen-like state identified by the fourteenth-century mystic Meister Eckhardt as *Gelassenheit*—a leaving behind, a forgetting, a losing, a loosening, a "releasement" from the idiom of self akin to that *Abgeschiedenheit*, or "detachment" equally vital to his practice of meditation and prayer. When Heidegger and Derrida come to discuss Eckhardt's apophatic theology, they both cite (as does Borges before them) Lehnert's favorite baroque poet, Angelus Silesius:

> *Die Ros' ist ohne warumb*
> *sie blühet weil sie blühet*

> *The Rose is without a why*
> *she blooms because she blooms*

> *Sie achtt nicht jhre selbst*
> *fragt nicht ob man sie sihet.*

She pays no mind to herself
nor asks if she be seen.

Not Gertrude's Stein's nominative "Rose is a rose is a rose," but rather a more Spinozan Rose, symbol of *natura naturans*, nature in its sheer event of naturing. And at the same time a Celanian *Niemandsrose*, ever blooming (like Eckhart's gnostic Godhead) as a Nobody addressed, intransitively, to No One.

Lehnert's Opus 8, *Wickerwork* is what he calls a Nature Book, a reading of the created world *sub specie aeternitatis*. In this it resembles some ancient *physiologus* or bestiary where the colorful catalogues of (pagan) animal or plant or mineral life are freighted with the moral and symbolic import of Christian myth. While lingering within this theological tradition of allegory, Lehnert at the same time casts a reverent scientist's eye on the five modern kingdoms of nature: plants, animals, fungi, protists (algae, amoebae) and monera (E. coli, bacteria), the minute particulars of which he often visually inspects as if under a microscope—as the child of two eye specialists, he had early dreams of becoming a microbiologist. Significantly enough, although his scalar Book of Nature contains (even in my abbreviated selection) various specimens of trees (16), birds (12), insects (12), as well as fish, invertebrates, amphibians, and various unicellular microorganisms, it features only two mammals—the bat and the whale, both honored for their uncanny poetic mastery of echolocation, finding their way by listening in. As for Man, he is a creature notably absent from Lehnert's *Naturae Liber*—even if the imprint of the human remains everywhere evident (and inevitable) in the anthropomorphic figures of personification and prosopopoeia that animate its poems. Thus the lowly (and very Blakean) Glowworm, so meager in sentience yet so apulse with the inner light of the divine:

> *I am blind of eye / I am deaf of ear /*
> *At dusk / the disembodied dust / shines near.*

Like many of the epigrams in the volume, this poem is simply entitled *Glühwürmchen* (*Lampyris noctiluca*) — the diminutive German noun first, followed by parenthetical Latin binomials (genus, species), in observance of the taxonomic system established by the Enlightenment botanist Linnaeus. In these titles, naming thus marks a site of translation, a threshold passage from the recognizable vernacular of the here and now into the remote auratic Latin of Linnaean infinitude. The illustrative epigrams incised below these hybrid titles—like the devices in emblem books—establish a similarly baroque interspace, filled with forms of life at once visible and invisible, reaching ever outwards and inwards, ever forwards and backwards, yet observed by a poet always aware (like Boehme) that even the loveliest signature of nature may but be the groundless afterimage or echo of a necessarily abyssal and unwritable God—or GOtt, as Lehnert and Sllesius prefer to spell it, splicing the upper and lowercase letters of the sacred tetragram JHWH (which I have in turn translated, following modern Jewish usage, as G-d).

The Jewish motifs in Lehnert's later poetry derive from the writings of Gershom Scholem on Lurianic Kabbalah, in particular his account of the doctrine of *tsimtsum*, the name for the self-eclipse of the Deity (*Ein Sof*) in his primal act of creation. By contracting himself, by withdrawing his fiery light into the void, his inner exile and concealment establishes that nothingness, or that infinite *within*, in which the finite world *without* can now come into being in the place thus left vacant or open by his disappearance, bounded in its free will (and attendant evil) only by his judgement and mercy (*din*). In an octave simply entitled "Tsimstum," Lehnert maps this cosmogonic event of creation *ex nihilo* onto a fleeting glimpse of the legendary salamander—ever reborn from its immunity to fire, ever regenerative of its limbs—who at the end of the poem silently slips away:

> *In the beginning / a heartbeat / the all in all*
> *Contracting / into itself / in a systole's twitch*
> *And quiver / suctioned into a warm cave /*
> *Now on its own / locked away / its blood*
> *Withstanding flame. But outside / nothing remains /*
> *Animal in stream / whirl of spades / scraping /*
> *The salamander escaping / its belly pulsating /*
> *Like glass / slipping off into the muddy grass.*

In the beginning (*bereshit*) was the heartbeat, its systole-diastole providing the pulse at the core of Creation—compared by Scholem to that ongoing process of divine inhalation and exhalation by which the breath of *ruah* (or *pneuma* or *anima* or spirit or wind) ebbs and flows throughout the world. Lehnert senses this primordial event of contraction and expansion, this ever-repeated rhythm of concealment and emanation, everywhere at work in the *Flechtwerk* of nature. He observes it in the undulations of the jellyfish (*Aurelia aurita*, or "gilded ear") as it withdraws into itself (or in German, herself) to find a path forward and outward:

> *. . . an echo of herself,*
> *forever the same, never too early*
> *or too late to venture out to sea*
> *as she journeys in, every contraction*
> *widening her sphere of action.*

He detects it in the constriction of the long-eared bat (*Plecotus auritus*) as it leaves its flights and listenings behind to retract into the restorative silence of prayerful hibernation:

> *Time frozen into frost / a dull pain / that congeals.*
> *Soon asleep / she'll shrivel into the spot / that heals.*

And he apprehends it in the migration of the brant goose, the ambit of whose wingbeats embraces a millennial glimpse of all that has been lost and all that might be saved:

> *She flees / without foresight / the year within her burden /*
> *The sea within her wingbeat / the once and coming / world.*

One of the corollaries of *tsimtsun*, according to Lurianic Kabbalah, was the catastrophic Breaking of the Vessels (or *Shevirat Ha-Kelim*) caused by the emanation of divine radiance over the course of the Creation. Given (to simplify drastically) that the space of finite matter was unable to contain the infinitude of holy fire thus poured into the narrow compass of its bowls, all the lower world could possibly hope to retain from this transcendent moment of inception was the memory of those primal seeds or sparks of divine light spilled and splintered throughout its shattered domain. The redemption from this fall from absent/present grace is known as *Tikkun*—that (ethical, ontological) promise of repair and restoration implied by the reintegration of exiled parts into their original whole. Drawing on this entire kabbalistic tradition, Lehnert develops a typically dense baroque conceit in his poem about the flowering mullein—known as King's Candle in German—a plant already recognized for its healing powers by Hippocrates and here presented as an allegory of *Tikkun*:

> *How find them again—all these fires*
> *Within matter / all these bright flashes of speech?*
> *Their nomen: King's Candles / wastelands beyond reach /*
> *Numen-like / Unmoored beacons of desire—*
> *Without syntax / or metaphor / unbroken by a breeze /*
> *Driven woodwards.*
> 　　　　　　　　*Shadow-yellow flames /*
> *Spirit spoken in tongues / wildfires / descended from the blaze—*
> *Echoed by a narrow clearing in the trees?*

In another poem explicitly entitled "The Breaking of the Vessels," Lehnert again stages the sudden emergence of a salamander:

> *It was too bright / there was a shattering of the light.*
> *A salamander's gleam / slithered through the pond.*

It, too, proceeds to vanish, leaving in its wake nothing but

> *Tiny bolts of lightning / driven / through the dark —*
> *The day / no more than / a dance of sparks.*

Finally, in a rare intrusion of the poet's lyrical I into these pages, Lehnert conjoins Jewish and Christian eschatology into a celebration of the messianic message offered by the scintillation of all these residues of the divine:

> *And the question grows / ever greater in the dark:*
> *What fuels the splendor / I bear within my heart?*
> *Was it kindled by something / tiny as a spark?*

*

THE SECOND BOOK HERE EXCERPTED from Lehnert's recent work is his earlier 2018 *Cherubinischer Staub* (or *Cherub Dust*), a title that alludes to Angelus Silesius's *Cherubinischer Wandersmann* (1674), a collection of devotional epigrams pseudonymously authored by Johann Scheffler in his persona as a cherubinic wanderer—or in Lehnert's case, as a contemporary backpacker sifting through the intermittent dust of angels. Again deploying the rhymed alexandrine distichs of the baroque era (here without slashes), Lehnert arranges his Basho-like (or Gary Snyder–like) treks through the valleys and mountains of what is sometimes called Saxon Switzerland into a kind of calendar poem (or *Kalendergedicht*) whose linked entries chronicle four seasons of spiritual errancy from the late fall of 2015 through the Advent Sundays of 2016, the onset of the liturgical year. Each of the epigrams is logged in by the precise date and geographical locus of its occurrence—and read quickly in succession, they register a pilgrim's jagged transit through what Emily Dickinson calls the inlets and outlets of the mind. Most of the poems take place in the vicinity of the poet's ramshackle farmhouse in Breitenau, a village situated just north of the Czech/Bohemian border in the midst of the Osterzgebirge (or Eastern Ore Mountains), while others are inspired by hikes along the Baltic shores of Caspar David Friedrich's Rügen or the V-2 proving grounds of Pennemünde. Whereas Lehnert's early poetry had ventured abroad into the wastes of the Sinai or the volcanic terrain of the Canary Islands in search of the sublime, here he sets out to discover the elusive visitations of the holy in the *Heimat* heart of the local.

Lehnert is sometimes seen as a distant descendent of the Saxon School of poets of the nineteen sixties and seventies. Drawing on the East German tradition of *Naturlyrik* already established by Johannes Bobrowski and Peter Huchel, such writers as Sarah Kirsch, Volker Braun, Heinz Czechowksi, and Wulf Kristen turned to landscape poetry during this Cold War period as a medium of political dissidence in which the environmental damage caused by the GDR's vaunted triumph over nature in the name of social and scientific progress (industrialized farming, monocultural forestry, secret uranium mining for the USSR) could be laid bare and critiqued. Among the more recent post-*Wende* East German poets, this turn toward the politically engaged environmentalism of *Ökolyrik* continues to make itself felt in the writings of two widely translated contemporary writers, Durs Grünbein and Lutz Seiler—both published, like Lehnert, by the prestigious (West German) house of Suhrkamp. Yet within this rich and ongoing tradition of German *Naturlyrik* and ecopoetry, Lehnert feels like something of an outlier. Given his theistic worldview, he objects to the species narcissism inherent in the notion of an Anthropocene era, and although in his writings he occasionally alludes to the despoliation of nature caused by centuries of extractive mining in the Ore Mountains (particularly tin and silver, the sources of the fabulous wealth of the Electors of Saxony) or to the infestation of bark beetles currently killing many of the local blue spruce forests planted by the government as acid rain resistant sources of industrial timber, the theophanic environmentalism of *Cherub Dust* feels almost premodern in its solitary encounters with the nonhuman.

What is above all striking about these locodescriptive calendar poems is the sheer intricacy of their craft. The first lines of each of these distichs kick off by condensing a range of natural events or processes into a mere twelve syllables: elder shrubs branching, spruce seeds splitting open, starlings gathering, pebbles whispering to clouds, snow thawing, ponds freezing over, tides ebbing back and forth—cross-sections or snapshots of nature in action. The initial six syllables of their second lines then shift from this world of verbs toward a lexicon of nouns, with each line initiated by the drone-like repetition of the German phrase "So heißt" (which I have translated "Thus the name of" or "Thus x is called")—an act of nomination that is immediately qualified (after an intervening colon) six syllables later by the metaphoric and/or metonymic predicates of thing thus christened (and hence promoted to a proper noun). The tripartite pulse of these serial rhymed couplets creates a cosmos of tiny infolded verse monads whose slightly offbeat logic (parts never quite subsumable into wholes) return the epigram to its distant origins in the gnomic practice of riddling—or to childhood memories of singsong nursery rhymes.

Although they are firmly anchored in the German genre of *Seelenlandschaft* (or "soulscape") poetry, I could not help but hear echoes of my own English-speaking tradition of nature writing as I listened in to Lehnert's splintered fragments. The following lines, for example, evoked Thoreau observing the surface of Walden Pond:

> *The waterskater skitters along the looking glass.*
> *So the sea by day is called: going nowhere fast.*

Or these, the memory of a Wordsworthian excursion along the strand:

> *Rilled ridges, a storm combing through the flatland.*
> *Thus my steady pace is named: cirrus wisps of sand.*

Or this, Shelley among the Euganean Hills:

> *The vista lost in all this mirrored glimmer.*
> *Thus rocks in bogs: a featherlight shimmer.*

Or (so often) Hopkins—the allusion to whose Windover became irresistible as I charted Lehnert's glimpse of a bird of prey from his attic window:

> *Morning's minion, the kite spirals into the wind.*
> *Thus early day is called: we're all woven in.*

Or this stray echo of Dickinson in Amherst, registering the first snowfall of the season in off-rhyme:

> *The spiderweb hangs riffled by an indifferent wind.*
> *First snow is named: what ever was, now must bend.*

*

THE SECOND SECTION OF *CHERUB DUST* consists of three dozen meditative couplets in which the poet's first person—now anxious, now ecstatic—at last edges more visibly into speech. In lines that achieve the laconic eloquence of Brecht's late *Bukower Elegies*, he notes down a brief moment of catharsis—that Heideggerian release of an Event or *Ereignis* whereby things suddenly emerge into their own by simply belonging together:

> *Cleansings, the sudden hail stones, the white lilies still upright*
> *in the lake, fleeting things, happening in plain sight.*

In another poem tellingly entitled "Epiphany," he manages to conjoin Hokusai and Mallarmé — the stillness of the symbolic swan only coming to be seen and heard — only coming into Being — as the after-effect of a retreating wave:

> *The swan touches the sea at that precise place of rest*
> *where the light is best seized — after wave crest.*

As he moves from one devotional distich to the next, Lehnert seeks out in every natural event the potential disclosure of a divine *advent*. Citing Isaiah's prediction that a shoot shall come forth from the stump of the Jesse tree, he reads in the veined signatures of its starlit leaves the prophetic script of a world redeemed. All one need do is look. And await:

> *Fragile leaves, veins more visible when sketched*
> *by starlight, when hoarfrost clings to tree's edge.*

And citing Romans (13:12) — "The night is far spent, the day is at hand: let us therefore cast off the works of darkness, and let us put on the armour of light"—he listens in to the landscape to locate the still small voice of a new—and utterly enigmatic—dawn.

> *I hear a sound, a low buzz in the scree,*
> *as though day had broken, with no reason to be.*

Richard Sieburth

Wickerwork

from OPUS 8. WICKERWORK
(2022)

A NATURE BOOK

Of Plants and Animals / Microbes and Stones of various Appearance /
Of their Names / Their Similitudes / Their Healing Powers / Their Breath /
Signatures in all their pulsating Motions / Vulnerable all of them /
And of the Ground of All the Above /
In all their Becoming and Extinction /
Soli Deo Gloria.

Montagu's harrier (Circus pygargus)

The harrier opens / to the storm / without a flicker of emotion.
Climbs a gust of wind / and settles into motion.

Die Wiesenweihe (Circus pygargus)

Die Weihe öffnet sich   dem Sturm / fast ohne Regung.
In Böen steigt sie auf   und ruht in der Bewegung.

The summer linden (Tilia platyphyllos)

The lung-tree / the linden / is breathing in.
The leaves quiver / and the wind drives home.
The tree lay far outside and within
The roots slept / their memory cast in stone:

There in its tousled hair the air has found a nest.
There night and day / have come to rest.
There the growth of things is never in doubt.
The linden / the lung-tree / is breathing out.

Die Sommerlinde (Tilia platyphyllos)

Der Lungenbaum / die Linde / atmet ein.
Die Blätter zittern / und der Wind dringt tief.
Weit draußen war der Baum und drinnen schlief
Die Wurzel / das Erinnern im Gestein:

Dort ist die Luft im Hargewirr zu Haus.
Dort ruhen / ungeschieden / Tag und Nacht.
Dort is das Wachsende schon stumm gedacht.
Der Lungenbaum / die Linde / atmet aus.

Glowworm (Lampyris noctiluca)

I am blind of eye / I am deaf of ear /
At dusk / the disembodied dust / shines near.

Glühwürmchen (Lampyris noctiluca)

Ich bin im Sehen blind / ich bin im Hören taub /
Vor mir im Dämmern glänzt ein körperloser Staub.

Flowering mullein (Verbascum densiflorum)

How find them again—all these fires
Within matter / all these bright flashes of speech?
Their nomen: King's Candles / wastelands beyond reach /
Numen-like / Unmoored beacons of desire—
Without syntax / or metaphor / unbroken by a breeze /
Driven woodwards.
                Shadow-yellow flames /
Spirit spoken in tongues / wildfires / descended from the blaze—
Echoed by a narrow clearing in the trees?

Großblütige Königskerze (Verbascum densiflorum)

Wie sie wiederfinden—diese Feuer
In den Stoffen / Blitz und helle Sprachen?
Namen: Königskerzen / trockne Brachen /
Numen waren's / Baken ohne Steuer—
Satzlos / Nicht Metaphern / nicht gebrochen —
Trieben waldwärts.
                Schattengelbe Flammen /
Geist in Zungen / Brand / dem sie entstammen—
Auf einer schmalen Lichtung nachgesprochen?

Icelandic moss (Cetraria islandica)

Its tongues lie soft / along gravel and growth ring.
Thus lichen flows / willing to want / nothing.

Isländisches Moos (Cetraria islandica)

Die Zungen liegen weich   auf Schotter und auf Schollen.
So fließen Flechten aus   im Willen / nichts zu wollen.

Grey geese breaking into flight

A leap / sheer wingbeat and alarm / not a word
Uttered / yet nothing quite itself from this point on:
The meadows taking fright around the pond /
The land disappearing / and the day unheard.

As I stood there in a formwork / a pain sliced
Through my knees / I saw wings rushing into flight
And bodies on the rise / thousands of cries /
Everything screaming / the light had been knifed.

Der Aufbruch der Graugänse

Ein Schwingen / Laut und Schwingenschlag / gesagt
War nichts / doch nichts blieb sich von nun an gleich:
Die Auen zitterten um einen Teich /
Dort war kein Land / dort war ein andrer Tag.

Ich stand in einer Schalung / einem Pochen /
Das in die Knie kroch / sah Flügel ragen /
Und Leiber stiegen auf / ein Tausendklagen /
Und alles schrie / das Licht war wie gestochen.

House martin (Delichon urbica)

The hatchling trips and falls. Its secure nest / vanishing from view /
Seized by the breezes / it no longer seeks / it finds anew.

Mehlschwalbe (Delichon urbica)

Das Junge zuckt und fällt. Was Nest war / Halt / verschwindet /
Die Böen greifen zu. Es sucht nichts mehr / es findet.

On sea cliffs

Mark well / it's all down in writing:
The rain upends a silvery leaf
And turns the page / and a tree shoot
Reads this and awaits. Chunks of chalk
Melt away / the tilted pine stands by
To ask for nothing more / to know nothing else /
In whatever happens / nothing's laid aside /
Mark / this pair of seagulls' cries.

An der Steilküste

Nun merke / es steht schon von allem geschrieben:
Der Regen bewegt ein silbriges Blatt
Und wendet es um / ein Stammschößling hat
Gelesen und wartet. Durchnäßt und zerrieben
Sind Kreiden / der kippende Baum ist bereit /
Nach nichts mehr zu fragen und nichts mehr zu wissen /
Was eben geschieht / enthält kein Vermissen /
Zu hören is nur / wie ein Möwenpaar schreit.

Hollyhock seed pods (Alcea rosea)

In a vase / time at rest / time set apart /
Future blossoms / the year cannot / take to heart.

Die Sammenkaspel der Stockrose (Alcea rosea)

In einer Schale ruht   die Zeit / von ihr getrennt /
Ein ferner Blütensog / das Jahr / das sie nicht kennt.

The creeping cinquefoil's seed (Potentilla reptans)

It knows of roots / it knows of pollen /
Of yellow fuzz / that sneaks up stalks /
Of leaves unscrolling as they open /
Of breathing skin / streaming into the dark.
It's borne in mind and is forgotten /
It's a body / it's a sign.
It's an echo / scattered to the wind.
It's a hand / that writes and writes.

Der Samen des Kriechenden Fingerkrauts (Potentilla reptans)

Er weiß die Wurzeln / weiß die Pollen /
Das Stengelkriechen / gelbe Matten /
Und wie sich öffnend Blätter rollen /
Die Atemhaut / verströmt im Schatten.
Er ist gedacht und ist entfallen /
Er ist ein Zeichen und ein Leib.
Er ist verweht / ein Widerhallen
Und Hand / die immer weiterschreibt.

The tinder fungus (Fomes fomentarius)

This trickle / this dim hum / of a world / in decay /
An old tree / listens for / what's rotting it away.

Der Zunderporling (Fomes fomentarius)

Das Rieseln / dies Gesumm   aus einer mürben Welt /
So lauscht der alte Baum   dem Anlaut / der ihn fällt.

Parmelia lichen (Parmelia physodes)

On this broken trunk / does it know its place
Or the body / into which it might extend?
Is it an outer sign / flecked with shade /
Or the rough tongue / of words beyond its ken?

Is it conscious of the light within?
Green that creeps / that forward slides?
Running riot / as it takes on time and stride /
Driving ever deeper into the foreign?

Die Schüsselflechte (Parmelia physodes)

Bruchholz / schwankend / weiß sie ihren Ort?
Ihren Körper / wohin will sie reichen?
Außen / schattenfleckig / ist sie Zeichen /
Harte Zunge / unbekanntes Wort.

Ob sie Licht im Inneren verspürt?
Grüne Schwebe / die sich vorwärts schiebt?
Wucherung / die Gang und Zeit ergibt /
Immer tiefer in die Fremde führt?

The tulip
or the opening of the rifts

She rises up red / like the fuse that drives lightning through a sea of
    clouds.
A rift: she breathes in / and the wind within her now gains ground.

Who is it / that smolders / magma-like or meteor-bright?
A rift: she breathes out / all body now / all pore and night.

Die Tulpe
oder Von den Spaltöffnungen

Rot zieht sie auf / verströmt / durchblitztes Wolkenmeer.
Ein Spalt: Sie atmet ein / der Wind wird in ihr schwer.

Wer ist es / der verglüht? Wie Magma / Meteore?
Ein Spalt: Sie atmet aus / wird Körper / Nacht und Pore.

White wagtail (Motacilla alba)

Forgotten—the steady wind / the flowerbeds lying fallow.
The whirr of its take-off / stirring the elder's shadow.

Bachstelzen (Motacilla alba)

Vergessen—steter Wind / die Beete liegen brach.
Die Stelzen schwirren auf / ein Erlenzweig wippt nach.

Brant goose (Branta bernicla)

She flees / without foresight / the year within her burden /
The sea within her wingbeat / the once and coming / world.

Die Ringelgans (Branta bernicla)

Sie flieht / schaut nicht voraus / sie trägt in sich das Jahr /
Im Schwingenschlag das Meer / die Welt / die wird und war.

The pensive hazel

She thinks and yearns / and stands in the wind
And hangs her concepts out in the winter sun.
Like little scrolls they slip her mind /
An imagined All / with a full run / of signs.
There were nights when she was snowblind /
Bare branches / where chance shapes spun.
Now she scatters pollen / getting wind
Of everything it was / she wished to send.

Die denkende Hasel

Sie denkt and sie begehrt / sie steht im Wind
Und hängt Begriffe in die Wintersonne.
Sie lösen sich von ihr / die Röllchen sind
Ein vorgestelltes All / darin geronnen /
Was sich ihr zeigte. Schneenachts war sie blind /
Ins Kahle / Zufallsformen eingesponnen.
Nun stäubt sie Pollen aus / und sie empfängt.
Herangeweht ist das / wohin sie drängt.

The eel (Anguilla anguilla)

The small pond at rest / only you brash enough / to find inflection /
As you slipstream along / stirring up / a direction.

Der Aal (Anguilla anguilla)

Der Weiher ruht / nur du bist lose / wirst zur Kraft /
Bewegst dich weiter / Sog / der ein Wohin sich schafft.

The night is far spent (Romans 13:12)

The herons with their silver throats /
The star that drives its pulse into the gravel
Around the icy stillness of the pool.
A path becomes clear / though it still leads to nothing /
Where shadow waits for light to give it form /
Where the word falls silent / ringing false within the void /
Where I make do without an inner home /
And fall like rime and gleam like stone.

Die Nacht ist vorgedrungen

Die silbrigen Hälse der Reiher /
In Kies senkt ein Stern seinen pulsenden Schein
An einem der froststillen Weiher.
Dort klärt sich ein Pfad / doch er führt noch ins Nichts.
Dort wartet ein Schatten auf formendes Licht.
Selbst Stille / das Wort ist verfälscht in der Leere /
Wo ich noch des inneren Ortes entbehre
Und falle als Rauhreif und leuchte als Stein.

Grass frog (Rana temporaria)

Like the glow of a glass vase / like the sheen / one forgets /
This smear of spawn upon the ground / doesn't exist / yet.

Die Grassfrösche (Rana temporaria)

Wie Glast und Glasgefäß / wie Schein / den man vergißt /
So schwebt der Laich am Grund / zu werden / was er ist.

Smoldering fire

I'm now at the turn / and here transpires
The far side of / what merely lives and dies.
Deep inside the eye / is this the site
Of the afterimage / that sets bush on fire?
Where night arises ever new from day /
And the question grows / ever greater in the dark:
What fuels the splendor / I bear within my heart?
Was it kindled by something / tiny as a spark?

Der Schwelbrand

Nun bin ich an der Kehre / hier beginnt
Die andre Seite dessen / was vergeht.
Pupilleninneres / woraus besteht
Das Nachbild / das in trocknem Reisig glimmt?
Wo aus dem Tag wird immer neu die Nacht /
Und in der Nacht wächst unentwegt die Frage:
Was nährt den Lichtschein / den ich in mir trage?
Ein Funkenflug / fast nichts / hat ihn entfacht?

Thyme (Thymus serpyllum)

Its scent / a shallow sleep / that seeps into the copse.
The heavy roots of light / sunk deep into the rocks.

Thymian (Thymus serpyllum)

Sein Duft / ein flacher Schlaf / versickert im Gestein.
Das wurzelschwere Licht   wächst in die Felsen ein.

Sycamore matter

It's different at different hours.
In the sun it exhibits / its split petioles /
Its sheets of bark / mushrooms in their folds /
Its blood scabbing the wounds of its roots.

At dusk it finally becomes clear. A tree born
Of itself / as rim and rift: Not what it is /
Grown so thick it makes a hole in the light /
Gone so dark / it waits at its own door.

Materie des Bergahorns

Er ist ein anderer zu andrer Stunde /
Zeigt Narbenschründe in der Sonne / Falten
Von Rindenschuppen / in verpilzten Spalten
Erstarrt das Baumblut aus den Wurzelwunden.

In Dämmern ist der Baum erst klar / ist Quelle
Von innen / Rand und Riß: Er ist es nicht /
Verdichtet sich zu einem Loch im Licht /
Wird schwarz / er steht an seiner eignen Schwelle.

With the skylark (Alauda arvensis)

To soar upward into sound / until all is lost /
Bereft of everything / the wind once bore aloft.

Mit der Feldlerche (Alauda arvensis)

Zu steigen in den Laut / bis alles sich verliert /
Bis nichts dein Eigen bleibt / der Wind dich erst gebiert.

Prayer with poppy

Not that anything / comes to pass
When we give You a name /
For the shape You take
Eludes our grasp.
Far clearer / from something to nothing /
So many things / ever the same /
Poppy blossoms / the falling light /
Sheathes of everything / lost and bright.

Mit dem Mohn gebetet

Nicht / daß es etwas gibt /
Wenn wir DIch nennen /
DEine Gestalt zerstiebt
Noch im Erkennen.
Klarer / von etwas zu nichts /
Vieles / und immer ist's eins /
Mohnblüten / fallendes Licht/
Häutchen verlorenen Scheins.

Blue algae (Cyanobacteria)

Sprung from the light / dressed in streaks
Of breath / inhaled from the innards / of the sea.

Die Blaualgen (Cyanobacteria)

Gewachsen aus dem Licht / in Schlieren ein Gewand
Aus Atem / der im Meer das Innere erfand.

The breaking of the vessels
or Of particulars

It was too bright / there was a shattering of the light.
A salamander's gleam / slithered through the pond.
A tiny sunstruck creature / quivered and spun
Its shingled skeleton / through the spawn.
A shimmer to the waves / as if the wind
Had gotten scent of life / so seaweed-green and soft.
Tiny bolts of lightning / driven / through the dark—
The day / no more than / a dance of sparks.

Der Bruch der Gefäße
oder Von den Einzelheiten

Es war zu hell / das Licht zersplitterte.
Ein Glasmolch schlüpfte / strahlte auf im Teich.
Ein Sonnentierchen kreiste / zitterte /
Sein Kiesskelett trieb schlingernd durch den Laich.
Ein Wellenflirren / so als witterte
Der Wind nach Leben / grün und algenweich.
Die feinsten Blitze / überall versunken—
So war der Tag nichts als ein Tanz von Funken.

Sweetwater polyp (Hydra)

What does the foot know of the ground? The Just Man stands in no-
man's land.
There he stands / shot through with / the good and the bad.

Der Süßwasserpolyp (Hydra)

Was weiß der Fuß vom Grund? Im Nichts steht der Gerechte.
Er steht und ihn durchdringt das Gute und das Schlechte.

Tsimtsum
or The young salamander's secret

In the beginning / a heartbeat / *the all in all*
Contracting / into itself / in a systole's twitch
And quiver / suctioned into a warm cave /
Now on its own / locked away / its blood /
Withstanding flame. But outside / nothing remains /
Animal in stream/ whirl of spades / scraping /
The salamander escaping / its belly pulsating /
Like glass / slipping off into the muddy grass.

Zimzum
oder Das Geheimnis des jungen Molches

Im Anfang ging ein Herzschlag. Krampfend zog
Sich *alles* / *das in allem war* / zusammen /
Ein Zucken / Winden / höhlenwarmer Sog /
Und war bei sich / verschloß sich / stand in Flammen
Und Blut. Doch draußen war es leer / dort wog
Ein Strom das Tier / ein Wirbeln / Schürfen / Schrammen.
Nur kurz sah ich den Bergmolch / dieses Pochen
Im Bauch wie Glas / sofort im Schlamm verkrochen.

Apollo butterfly pupa (Parnassius apollo)

She perishes / and comes to rest / inside a cocoon.
A forgotten figure / awakened to the night / within her room.

Puppe des Apollo (Parnassius apollo)

Zugrunde geht sie / ruht   in ein Gespinst gebracht.
Vergessene Gestalt   erwacht in ihrer Nacht.

E-coli (Escherichia coli)

"So cozy are space and time / these vessels that live for my good /
who rescue and carry me / to where I float about in food."

Das Kolibakterium (Escherichia coli)

"So warm sind Raum und Zeit /   Gefäß / das für mich lebt /
Mich birgt und dorthin trägt /   wo Nahrung mich umschwebt"

The canny amoeba

What turns up outside / be it substance or reflection /
Flows around the cell / its pseudopod extended / in affection.

Die erkennende Amöbe

Was sich da draußen zeigt / ob Stoff / ob Widerschein /
Umfließt ihr Zellfuß / greift und holt es in sie ein.

Toad larvae (Bufo bufo)

A teeming mass / a suction pool / mouths that snap
At algae / the tadpoles' Lenten veil / woven black.

Erdkrötenlarven (Bufo bufo)

Gewimmel ohne Maß / ein Sog / die Mäuler schnappen
Nach Algen / weben schwarz   das Hungertuch der Quappen.

Viruses

Leftover lives / it's only on others they take their chance /
These tiniest of souls / ever restless for foreign lands.

Viren

Ein Überrest / sie sind   am Leben nur in andern /
der Seelen winzigste /   die durch die Fremde wandern.

Trumpet animalcule (Stentor)

Here again / the tiniest of specificities /
Powered through the slime to strips of peat:
A manner of eyelash / an awl in algae loop /
All pulse all weave / in bark skin sheathed /
A quick breath / aquiver / in a droplet's throat /
A high note drawn from water / slime and time /
A gorge and whirlpool / dipped in brine /
Lasting only so long / as it flows inside.

Das Trompetentierchen (Stentor)

Noch mehr und winzigste der Einzelheiten /
Auf Fasern Torf im Faulschlamm angetrieben:
Ein Wimpernstil / ein Pfriem im Algenschlingern /
Er pulst und schwankt / von Rindenhaut umschrieben /
Im Tröpfchenhals vibriert ein schneller Hauch /
Ein hoher Ton aus Wasser / Fett und Zeit /
Ein Schlund und Strudel / in den Bach getaucht /
Beständig nur / indem es strömt im Inneren.

Moon jellyfish (Aurelia aurita)

A scalloped saucer / its mucus dome / reminding the sea
Of all the umbrellas it forgot to take / when leaving home.

Ohrenqualle (Aurelia aurita)

Ein Schwingen / Wellenkreis / in dem das Meer erkennt:
In seiner Strömung schwimmt ein früherer Moment.

Elvers

Headed home and knowing not where /
The elvers swim this swift stream like glass /
And growing larger / their darkness blurs
Their yellow bellies / into a snake's mass.
Are they remembered? By whom? The dream
That possessed them / will it begin anew?
Weighted down by another black reverie
Hidden in muck / they teem / they seek / they skew.

Die jungen Aale

Sie kehren heim und wissen nicht wohin.
In einem schnellen Strom sind sie wie Glas
Und wachsen / ihre Dunkelheit gerinnt
Vom gelben Bauch her / findet Schlangenmaß.
Sind sie erinnert? Doch von wem? Beginnt
Ein Traum von neuem / der sie schon besaß?
Sie werden schwer in einem schwarzen andern /
Im Schlamm versteckt / und wimmeln / suchen / wandern.

Potato sprout

A long pale tendril / feeling its way through the dark
To get a sense / of what it was / that never left a mark.

Der Kartoffelkeim

Ein fahler langer Arm / der sich ins Dunkel schmiegt /
Ertastet / was es sei / wass dort vergessen liegt.

Digging

The unshaped / softness / of the damp soil
That absorbs everything / being nobody's foe
And nobody's form.   You plant the spuds /
Their sprouts as glassy / as diodes' glow—
The soil could care less / what touches it.
As far as it's concerned / everything derives
From the selfsame sun / even lime / even the wide
Dire post-hole leading down to cold loam.

Umgraben

Das Weiche / ungestalt / der feuchte Boden
Nimmt alles in sich auf / ist niemands Feind
Und niemands Form. Du furchst Kartoffeln ein /
Die Keime / glasig / leuchten wie Dioden—
Ihm ist es gleich / wie alles / was ihn rührt.
Denn von der einen Sonne abgeleitet /
Scheint alles ihm / auch Kalk / auch angstgeweitet
Das Pfahlloch / das in kalten Lehmgrund führt.

Oxlip (Primula elatior)

Primrose by the creek / entrusted to the sun's care /
Rising into air. You know not / what it seeks.

Hohe Schlüsselblume (Primula elatior)

Am Bach ein Schlüsselbart / den sich die Sonne schleift /
Regt in die klare Luft. Du weißt nicht / wo er greift.

Black elderberry (Sambucus nigra)

Hands off the elder / touch not this shrub
At the corner of the wall / where the wind
Gets cut and tossed / for its branches hug
The house / to keep it from getting lost.

Forms like you / a wisp of smoke /
A pillar risen before the storm—
Elder breath / burns poorly / a bitter weed
That shoots forth with us / and joins us in the freeze.

Der Holunderbusch (Sambucus nigra)

Quäle nie den Holder / nicht den Strauch
An der Mauerecke / wo der Wind
Blank zerschnitten wird / die Zweige sind
Halt dem Haus / daß es sich nicht verliert.

Formen wie du selbst / so geht ein Rauch /
Eine Säule steht vor dem Gewitter—
Holderhauch / es brennt schlecht / ist ein Bitter-
Kraut / das mit uns aufgeht / mit uns friert.

The autumn spider

Knows not / who she is / and has eaten / all she earned.
In her web / she lies in wait / for memories / to return.

Die Herbstspinne

Sie weiß nicht / wer sie ist / hat / was es gab / verschlungen.
Sie lauert nun im Netz / auf die Erinnerungen.

Poppy (Papaver rhoeas)

The poppy bobs and bends / in the wind / beckoning the flies
Aboard / to rock themselves back / into its cradle of fire.

Mohn (Papaver rhoeas)

Der Mohn wippt / und er nickt   im Wind / er winkt den Fliegen /
Sie kommen / fühlen sich   in Flammen wie in Wiegen.

Red wood ants (Formica rufa)

Their nest extends / the full length of the branch
That breaks / handing the ants / over to chance.

Die Waldameisen (Formica rufa)

Ein meterlanger Leib   kriecht schlängelnd ins Geäst /
Wo er zerfällt und sich   dem Zufall überläßt.

Eyed hawk-moth (Smerinthus ocellata)

The sunlight darkens / into the red embers of the trees.
Two eyes open / and the night grows / into what they see.

Abendpfauenauge (Smerinthus ocellata)

Ein dunkles Sonnenlicht / die Glut ist rot entfacht.
Zwei Augen öffnen sich / dort wächst im Blick die Nacht.

Crowflight

The fog rolls in / they sharpen their claws /
They flock into balls / and have a great fall.

Krähenflug

Die Nebel werden fest / sie schärfen ihre Krallen /
Sie ballen sich im Schwarm / sie strömen aus und fallen.

Rowanberry (Sorbus acucuparia)

All the bitterness / all the reds / of summers long ago—
The berries taking on a glow / as thicket welcomes snow.

Vogelbeere (Sorbus acucuparia)

Die Bitterkeit / das Rot / das lang vom Sommer bleibt—
Die Beeren leuchten auf / wenn Schnee durchs Dickicht treibt.

Winter bees

All abuzz / clinging to each other / as they swarm.
A moment's anxiety / all you need / to keep forever warm.

Winterbienen

Sie schwirren / klammern sich am andern fest / im Schwarm.
Die Angst / minutenlang /   hält für Minuten warm.

The silver fir (Abies alba)

She finally fell asleep / under the weight / of all the snow.
A peace this deep / beyond anything / ever wished or known.

Die Weißtanne (Abies alba)

Die Schneelast wurde schwer /　die Tanne schlief und schwankte.
Die Ruhe drang so tief /　wie sie noch nie gelangte.

Walnuts

They take a deep breath: Everything outside themselves
Goes numb / goes mute / cold and invisible / as shells.

Walnüsse

Sie atmen langsam ein: Was außen war / erstarrt /
Verstummt / zerfällt / zerfriert / wird unsichtbar und hart.

White birch (Betula pubescens)

Set in mud / she sprouts and roots / until the blight.
Her growth is stones / dancing with the light.

Die Moorbirke (Betula pubescens)

Sie keimt und steht im Sumpf /   treibt Wurzeln / bis sie bricht.
Ihr Wachsen ist ein Tanz   der Steine mit dem Licht.

Plankton
Driven this way and that

The Creator / a stream / too pure for home—
Should you plan to dwell in it / prepare to roam.

Plankton
Die Umhergetriebenen

Der Schaffende / ein Strom / so unbewohnbar rein—
Wer in ihm hausen will / muß ohne Bleibe sein.

Sphere algae (Volvox)

A film of green / a membrane / its origin lost in time /
Its yesterdays and tomorrows / sheathed in slime.

Kugelalgen (Volvox)

Ein grüner Film / Membran / sein Ursprung ist verborgen /
In Trübung eingehullt / in Gestern und in Morgen.

The whale

The major third seeks whom? Where's the interval's place?
The blue whale sings at night / in the mists of inner space.

Der Wal

Wen sucht die große Terz?   Was meint das Intervall?
Der Blauwal singt bei Nacht   mit Nebeln tief im All.

Amethyst

A sleeping beauty's afterblush? The amethyst
dreams / of the roar / and hush / and pulse of waves
as strands of kelp / swell and slosh
against the cliff /
                    And listens to the hiss
of foam / as it disintegrates. Or to a cyclone
in whose eye / time has lost its way / or to a stone
hollowed out / and draped with quartz / in whose geode
in whose tone / it now proceeds / to grow.

Der Amethyst

Ein Nachglanz? Langer Schlaf? Im Amethyst
Geht unentwegt ein Rauschen / pulsen Wellen
Voll Algenschlieren / ebben ab und schwellen
Und fluten gegen Klippen.
                          Hörbar ist /
Wie Schaum zerfällt. Ein drehender Zyklon /
In seiner Mitte ist die Zeit vergangen /
Ist Hohlgestein geworden / quarzverhangen /
Dort wächst der Amethyst aus seinem Ton.

The butterbur (Petasites hybridus)
or The memory plant

This the enigma: Of all the dogged / lilac names
Of the dead / this blossom tells / their escape.

Pestwurz (Petasites hybridus)
oder Das Erinnerungskraut

Es gibt das Enigma: Geballt / die lila Namen
Der Toten / Blütensproß erzählt / wie sie entkamen.

Pair of blackbirds
Intent on changing nests

Their exit too weak / two tired smudges side by side /
Mere bodies on the line / what they're sick of / what they hide.

Das Amselpärchen
Wie es von seinem Nest ablenkt

Zu schwach / ein Niederschlag zwei müde schwarze Flecken?
Sie spielen nur den Leib / das Kranksein / das Verstecken.

Aspen (Populus tremula)

Quaking aspen / its days counted / its foliage / at an end.
A single leaf / broken free / follows its bent / in pale descent.

Espe (Populus tremula)

Sie zittert / längst gezählt ist alles Laub / vollendet.
Das abgebrochne Blatt weiß fallend sich gewendet.

Windgrass *(Apera spica-venti)*

No mortal word / can measure / what blows away.
The wind in the grass / recites / what remains.

Ackerwindhalm *(Apera spica-venti)*

Kein Sterbenswörtchen nimmt an dem Verwehen Maß.
Was unvergänglich ist / erzählt der Wind im Gras.

Long-eared bat (Plecotus auritus) before hibernation

Time frozen into frost / a dull pain / that congeals.
Soon asleep / she'll shrivel into the spot / that heals.

Großohr (Plecotus auritus) vor der Winterruhe

Die Zeit erstarrt im Frost / ein Schmerz / der dumpf verweilt.
Bald schläft sie / schrumpft zum Punkt in ihm / wo sie verheilt.

Names

The name is an herb / a seedling and a shaft /
Risen from the sound / of wood and oil and sap.

Namen

Der Name ist ein Kraut / ein Keimling und ein Schaft /
Gewachsen aus dem Laut / zu Holz und Öl und Saft.

Herbs

A name is the herb / imagined by the silent seed /
Forgotten beneath the snow / realized by sprout and leaf.

Kräuter

Ein Name ist das Kraut / im Samen stumm gedacht /
Vergessen unterm Schnee / in Keim und Blatt gebracht.

The fossil

White stone / with an animal trace / greeting us
With a face / as tender as a fetus.

Das Fossil

Ein weißer Stein / darin   die Zeichnung / sie bewahrt
Gewesenes / ein Tier /   noch wie ein Fötus zart.

Ground beetle (Carabus auronitens)

From what he sees and smells / before reaching the river of tar /
Step by step / he knows for certain / it can't be far.

Goldglänzender Laufkäfer (Carabus auronitens)

So weit er sieht und riecht / bis er am Teerfluß steht /
So weiß er Schritt für Schritt   Bescheid und geht und geht.

Before the storm

Approaching faster / than wild carrots
Wilt / or lily leaves rot in bog /

Or rocks that hum and run amuck /
Far better / to disturb nothing in the haze /
And keep an ear out / for what this enchanted place

Asks: What is the sense / that drives you to be safe?
Blinded by fog / how still find your way?
The very path that now appears / where it went astray?

Vor dem Unwetter

Dorthin / schneller / wo die wilden Möhren
Welken / wo das Lilienlaub im Moor

Zerfällt / und summend dringt Geröll hervor /
Und besser ist es / nichts im Dunst zu stören /
Zu lauschen / was es fragt / gereiztes Land:

Was ist der Sinn / der dich ins Sichre führt?
Wenn nebelblind du doch die Richtung spürst?
Derselbe Pfad taucht auf / wo er verschwand?

from CHERUB DUST
(2018)

Oktober 2015, Breitenau, Osterzgebirge

Ein Rauhreif, abends haucht das Kind auf schwarzes Glas.
So wird der Schwan genannt: die Stille ohne Maß.

Vierundzwanzigster Oktober 2015, Breitenau ·

Die letzte Ästelung, das Haar, das Wurzel-Wort.
So heißt der Holderstrauch: mein eingehauchter Ort.

October 2015, Breitenau, Eastern Ore Mountains

Hoarfrost, evening, a child's breath on black glass.
Thus the name of the swan: stillness without mass.

October twentyfourth, 2015, Breitenau

The final branching, the hair, the root sense.
Thus the elder shrub is called: my place of breath.

Ende Oktober 2015, Oehlsengrund, Osterzgebirge

In Spätherbst, Flammenhang, die Sonne wärmt nicht mehr.
So heißt das Eichenlaub: Die Lider werden schwer.

Januar 2016, Achterwasser, Usedom

Er löst sich lautlos auf, ins Wasser sinkt der Schnee.
So wird der Schlaf genannt: die unerforschte See.

End of October 2015, Oehlsengrund, Eastern Ore Mountains

Late fall, slope in flames, the sun no longer warming.
Thus the name of oak leaves: eyelids in mourning.

January 2016, Achterwasser, Usedom

A silent thaw, the snow watery, less awake.
Thus sleep is called: an unsuspected lake.

Januar 2016, Usedom

Gezeiten schwingen fort, im Eis hörst du das Pochen.
So wird der Frost genannt: die Angst der Nagelrochen.

Dreizehnter Februar 2016, Breitenau

Ein Summen, tief im Holz, das in die Silben fährt.
So wird die Glut genannt: der Stoff, der Namen nährt

January 2016, Usedom

Back and forth of tides, you hear knocks in the ice.
Thus the name of frost: a sea skate taking fright.

February thirteenth 2016, Breitenau

Something buzzing in the tree, syllables for sure.
Thus the name for embers: matter feeding words.

Vierzehnter Februar 2016, Breitenau

Das klare Wasser friert vom Rand her in die Quelle.
So heißt der Mittagsfrost: Wir harren auf der Schwelle.

Ostern 2016, Hennersbach, Osterzgebirge

Die Stare sammeln sich im dürren Laub der Schlehen.
So heißt der Pfad am Berg: Aus Staub wirst du erstehen.

February fourteenth 2016, Breitenau

The water's frozen clear from shore to spring.
Thus the name of noonday frost: waiting at the brink.

Easter 2016, Henner's Creek, Eastern Ore Mountains

The starlings gather mid the spindled blackthorn spikes.
Thus the mountain path is called: from dust shalt thou arise.

Fünfzehnter Mai 2016, am Oberlauf der Seidewitz,
Osterzgebirge

Die Kiesel flüstern nachts die Wolkennamen nach.
So heißt der Stein im Fluß: Die Stunden liegen brach.

Ende Mai 2016, Pfarrwald in Breitenau

Im Unterholz, im Farn verwuchern mir die Sinne.
So heißt der Fichtenkeim: das staunende Beginnen.

May fifteenth 2016, on the high trail of the Seidewitz,
Eastern Ore Mountains

At night the pebbles whisper to the names of clouds.
Thus stone in stream is called: the hours lying there unplowed.

End of May 2016, Pfarr Forest in Breitenau

My senses stifled by all the underbrush and bracken.
Thus the name of the spruce seed: amazed, it happens.

Mitte Mai 2016, am Feldrand in Breitenau

Du schaust den Schwalben nach, den Schatten, die verrauschen.
So heißt der erste Vers: Geräusch des eignen Lauschens.

Ende Mai 2016, Moorgründe am Sattelberg, Osterzgebirge

Mit vollen Blättern glänzt der Sonnentau den Fliegen.
So heißt die Süßigkeit: Ein Echo will mich wiegen.

Mid-May 2016, at meadow's edge in Breitnau

You observe all the swallows and shadows growing dim.
Thus the first line is named: the sound you make, listening in.

End of May 2016, marshes near the Sattelberg, Eastern Ore Mountains

Amid the leaves, the gleam of sun-thaw on the flies.
Thus the name of sweetness: an echo, my rock-a-bye.

Achtzehnter Juni 2016, vor den Walzenornamenten, Breitenau

Die Ranken an der Wand, das Muster gleicht sich immer.
So heißt die Zukunft tags: das unbegrenzte Zimmer.

Achtzehnter Juni 2016, im Ostwind über die Höhen

Ein Sturm umkreist das Haus, Geräusch von überall.
So heißt die Zukunft nachts: der Hang im freien Fall.

June eighteenth 2016, wooden wall ornaments, Breitenau

The tendrils on the walls, always identical in design.
Thus the name of the future by day: a room with no sides.

June eighteenth 2016, in the eastwind over the heights

Storm sweeping around the house, noise pouring in.
Thus the name of the future by night: free fall from a cliff.

Neunzehnter Juni 2016, Schlottwitzer Bruch im Müglitztal

Sekundenschlaf, ein Riß durchzieht den Fels, verwittert.
So heißt der Amethyst: Der Bodensatz erzittert.

Ende Juni 2016, Dünen auf dem Darß

Gewellter Grund, ein Sturm verschleift das flache Land.
So heißt mein fester Gang: die feinen Zirren Sand.

June nineteenth 2016, Schlottwitzer Notch in the Müglitz Valley

Split-second of sleep, a rip through weather-worn rock,
Thus the name of amethyst: sediment in shock.

Late June 2016, dunes on the Darss

Rilled ridges, a storm combing through the flatland.
Thus my steady pace is named: cirrus wisps of sand.

Dritter Juli 2016, am Dachfenster, Breitenau

Des Morgens Glück, Milan, kreist mit dem Wind nach oben.
So heißt der frühe Tag: Wir werden eingewoben.

Fünfter Juli 2016, Bergwiese bei Gottgetreu, Osterzgebirge

Ein Flackern, doch nichts brennt, in Sumpf und Wiesenfeuchten.
So heißt der schwarze Storch: ein inwendiges Leuchten.

July third 2016, at the attic window, Breitenau

Morning's minion, the kite spirals into the wind.
Thus early day is called: we're all woven in.

July fifth 2016, mountain meadow near Gottgetreu,
Eastern Ore Mountains

A flicker of flame, but no fire on marsh or meadow.
Thus the black stork's name: an inward glow.

Achter Juli 2016, Peenemündung

Der Wasserläufer zuckt auf einem Spiegel hin.
So heißt das Meer am Tag: der umgekehrte Sinn.

Zehnter Juli 2016, Dahmer Kanal

Im Torf die Quelle kennt in Klarheit kein Verlangen.
So heißt das Augenschwarz: das leuchtende Empfangen.

July eighth 2016, Peenemündung

The waterskater skitters along the looking glass.
So the sea by day is called: going nowhere fast.

July tenth 2016, Dahmer canal

Peatbog brook has little reason to run bright.
Thus the name for eyeblack: embrace the light.

Anfang September 2016, im Laternenlicht, Breitenau

Im Husch vorbei—ein Ruf? Ein Sirren oder Wimmern?
So heißt die Fledermaus: verspätetes Erinnen.

September 2016, Nebel über den Hochwiesen am Sattelberg

Nichts ordnet mehr die Sicht, den spiegelhellen Glimmer.
So heißt der Fels im Moor: ein federleichter Schimmer.

Early September 2016, in the lamplight, Breitenau

Whoosh—a call? A bang or whimper in fact?
Thus the name of the bat: the afterthought of that.

September 2016, fog over the high meadows on the Sattelberg

The vista lost in all this mirrored glimmer.
Thus rocks in bogs: a featherlight shimmer.

Oktober 2016, Gottleubatal, Osterzgebirge

Verloren, wie das Laub, sind Namen, die wir hatten.
So heißt das Buchenrot: des Sommers lange Schatten.

Ende Oktober 2016, am Sattelberg

Das Moos wächst unbeirrt, als wüßte es, wohin.
So heißt das tote Holz: im Sumpf der Richtungssinn.

October 2016, Gottleuba Valley, Eastern Ore Mountains

Lost, like the leaves, those names by which we went.
Thus red beech is called: shadow of a summer spent.

End of October 2016, on the Sattelberg

Moss knows well where it'll extend, section by section,
Thus the name of dead wood: no sense of direction.

November 2016, Lärchenschlag, Breitenau

Gewirr und später Wuchs, der Waldrand ist vermessen.
So heißt das Flechtengrau: das samtene Vergessen.

Erster Advent 2016, Autobahn vor Breitenau

Ein Rauhgefieder treibt, es weiß den Weg nicht mehr.
So heißt der Nebelgang: Gezeiten ohne Meer.

November 2016, clear cutting of larches, Breitenau

The forest is surveyed, to check its sprawl from spreading.
Thus the name of lichen grey: the velvet of forgetting.

First Advent 2016, Autobahn by Breitenau

The wings, raw with wind, no longer know their reach.
Thus the name of the fogs rolling in: tides with no beach.

Neunundzwanzigster November 2016, Breitenau

Ein unentwegter Wind bewegt die Spinnenweben.
So heißt der erste Schnee: Was immer war, soll schweben.

Zweiter Advent 2016, Breitenau

Die Wörter bleiben still, sie wollen nirgendshin.
So heißt die Müdigkeit: der schweigende Beginn.

Twenty-ninth November 2016, Breitenau

The spiderwebs hang riffled by an indifferent wind.
First snow is named: what ever was, now must bend.

Second Advent 2016, Breitenau

The words hold still, there's nowhere they want in.
Thus the name of fatigue: in silence it begins.

Elfter Dezember 2016, Leipzig

Die Krähen wiegen sich im Schnee und schreien irr.
So heißt das letzte Blatt: der Satz im Lautgewirr.

* * *

December eleventh 2016, Leipzig

In the snow the crows rock back and forth, cawing off key.
Thus the name of the final leaf: sentences that don't agree.

* * *

Tierhaft

Allein in das Gesträuch, nun ohne Richtungssinn,
geduckt, so hab ich Zeit, weil ich ein Echo bin.

Sturm

Ein dichter Schnee, in mir die Atemnot, so klingt
der GOtt, ein feiner Zweig, der zittert, summt und schwingt.

Animal-like

Crouched in the bushes, now past my prime.
A passing echo, I have the time.

Storm

The snow lies deep, I need to breathe, this is what G-d
sounds like—a spindled branch, a shiver, a hum, a nod.

Böhmischer Wind über der Autobahn, Breitenau

Hydraulisch, Gleitschub, schrill—die Nacht is frostgetrocknet
und bebt, ein Zeitenriß, aus Sternen wehen Flocken.

Traum

"Anderwelt"—ein Wort, weist den Weg hinüber,
fordert: fort, nur fort, schenkt dir ein Gefieder.

Wind out of Bohemia over the Autobahn, Breitenau

Hydraulic brakes, careening sideways, night road frozen hard,
a crash, a rip in time, snowflakes drifting down from stars.

Dream

"Otherworld"—the word points to what the path might bring.
Thus urged onward, award yourself extended wings.

Und es wird ein Reis hervorgehen

Brüchiges Laub, die Adern, Zeichnungen zeigen sich klarer
nach der Sternennacht, Reif auf dem Wurzelarm.

Neuschnee

Die Wehe, windgenährt, weich an das Haus gedrückt—
nach jedem Gang ist's still, ein Anfang kehrt zurück.

And there shall come forth a rod out of the stem (Isaiah 11:1)

Fragile leaves, veins more visible when sketched
by starlight, when hoarfrost clings to tree's edge.

Fresh snow

The snowdrift, fed by the wind, eases up against the hut,
goes silent after every gust, rebeginning as it must.

Aufgetauter Tümpel

Dies Auge, es entfiel dem GOtt in seinem Schweben.
Es sieht nun auf, ER schaut das ungeschaffne Leben.

Die Nacht ist vorgedrungen

Ich höre ein Geräusch, ein Sirren im Gestein,
als sei der Tag schon wach und darf doch noch nicht sein.

Thawed pond

As G-d hovered in the balance, He let fall
this eye, now peering up to espy the uncreated All.

The night is far spent (Romans 13:12)

I hear a sound, a low buzz in the scree,
as though day had broken, with no reason to be.

Puls

Der GOtt wird nicht gedacht, im Atem wird ER wahr.
So hebt im Dunkel an, des Nachts, das neue Jahr.

Wandlung

Der graue Schnee zerrinnt, er nährt den Schlamm, er dringt
ins Erdreich ein und lauscht, wie jede Pore klingt.

Pulse

G-d is not something thought, but in breath becomes real.
In the dark of night, a new year is revealed.

Transformation

The grey snow melts away, feeds the mud, and pours
into the soil, lending an ear to every spore.

Tag- und Nachtgleiche

Der Schmetterling im März, noch winterklamm, will schwirren.
Was ist für ihn die Zeit? Ein Flügelschlag und Irren?

Engelsgeräusch

> "Quem quaeritis in speulchro?"
> (Tropus der Osternacht)

Was sucht ihr hier im Grab? Den Wind und Echoklang,
den Zungenlaut am Grat zum warmen Höhlengang.

Equinox

March butterfly, still numb with winter, wanting flight at any cost.
What's time to him? A wingbeat, and then get lost?

The rustle of an angel

> "Quem quaeritis in sepulchro?"
> (Easternight trope)

For what are you searching in this tomb? For the wind's and echo's wake?
For the sound the tongue doth make, climbing this ridge to the warm cave?

Birkenwasser

Die junge Birke ist im Bluten eine Frage
nach einem Ganzen, nach der Richtung ihrer Klage.

Auge des Sturms

Das Wimmern in der Luft, also sei der Wind verletzt
und schleppt sich aus der Welt—er atmet ein zuletzt?

Birch water

The blood of the young birch is a question meant
for the whole, for the full extent of her lament.

Eye of the storm

This whimpering in the air, as if the wounded gale
Were slinking from the earth—yet in the end inhaled.

Muttersprache

Das Zimmer, wo du schreibst, wird nächtlich abgerissen,
verbrannt in einer Glut, im wortlosen Vermissen.

Der eigene Ton

Ein Fremder wachte auf, er sprach dieselben Dinge
und irrte so wie ich, hofft, daß ich in ihm schwinge.

Mother tongue

The room in which you write gets torn away at night
and burned up in the fire, out of words, out of sight.

The personal note

A stranger awoke, saying the same sorry things
as me, in the hope I'd lend him my wings.

Im Erwachen

Noch ist der Tastsinn fremd, ist außen noch kein Raum:
Ich bin ein Gliedertier in seinem Muscheltraum.

Urwort

Wer fand zuerst ein Wort wie "Schaumkraut", Wellennamen?
Ein Wind kam auf und trug bei Nacht heran die Samen.

Upon waking

The sense of touch still strange to me, no space out there in which
    to dwell:
I'm a creature possessed of limbs, yet dream like a mussel in its shell.

Primal word

Who first called bittergrass by the marine name "foamweed"?
A wind arose at night and floated forth its seed.

Ins Offene

Das Brennesselgesträuch wächst dicht nach allen Seiten,
kennt keinen Weg, nur Raum, den Wurzeln suchend weiten.

Im Schatten

Innerhalb weniger Tage verwuchert der Wald in sein Dämmern.
Bodennah wächst nur noch Kraut, das sich selber genügt.

Into the open

The nettle bush grows thick, everywhere on the loose,
Needing no path, just room to envisage further roots.

In the shade

It takes but a few days for the woods to go dark and overgrown.
The forest floor all weeds, down there on their own.

Wo ist GOtt?

Das Undeutliche, GOtt, kann dies und jenes sein.
Wo immer du IHn suchst, schließt ER dich in sich ein.

Epiphanie

Der Schwan berührt das Meer genau an jener Stelle,
wo Licht verstanden wird, die brandungslose Welle.

Where is G-d?

G-d, inscrutable, can be either this or that thing.
Wherever you search for Him, He takes you in.

Epiphany

The swan touches the sea at that precise place of rest
where the light is best seized—after wave crest.

Von fern

Es gibt den Bergmolch noch, in einem Teich erinnert,
der rote Kamm, der nur dem Absichtslosen schimmert.

Es gibt IHn nicht

Es gibt nicht "GOtt", es spricht ein unentwegtes Geben,
in dem ER selber wird, in Dasein und Entschweben.

From afar

The Alpine newt still exists, remembered in a small lake,
its red comb only clear to one with nothing at stake.

He doesn't exist

"G-d" doesn't exist, what speaks is an unswerving gift
in which He becomes what He is, as off He drifts.

Proömium

Läuterungen, das sind der plötzliche Graupel, die weißen
Lilien, aufrecht am See, Flüchtiges, wie es geschieht.

Das Jenseits der Fische

In allen Körpern hängt ein Beutel Fremde, trocken
und leer. In Schwebe hält er Schwimmende wie Flocken.

Proem

Cleansings, the sudden hail stones, the white lilies still upright
in the lake, fleeting things, happening in plain sight.

Far side of fish

A pouch of something strange hangs in everyone like an ache,
Dry and empty, holding floating things at bay like tiny flakes.

Ruhendes Jetzt

Die Apfelblüte fällt, verwelkt, kehrt nie zurück.
Du findest dich in ihr für einen Augenblick

Völliges Dunkel

Im Nachtwind lösen sich die leichten Espenzungen,
zu flüstern. Unsichtbar wird nun ein Baum gesungen.

Now at rest

The apple blossom falls, fades, with this you can never reckon,
yet find yourself within it for a never-ending second.

Total dark

In the nightwind the frail aspen tongues
begin to whisper. A tree, invisible, shall now be sung.

Nachtfalter

Der Pappelschwärmer läßt sich tags entseelt bewegen,
wie eine Zeichnung, wie sich Bilder niederlegen.

Totenkopfschwärmer (Acherontia atropos)

Der Weg ist plötzlich fremd. Ob ihn ein Falter träumt?
Der nachts auf Zäunen hockt und alles Leben säumt?

Moth

The hawkmoth allows its soulless self to quiver during the day
like a drawing, like an image pinned upon a page.

African death's head hawkmoth (Acherontia atropos)

The path suddenly seems strange. Is this a butterfly's dream?
Who alights on fences at night, mending life's seams?

Der Übergang

Der immer gleiche Pfad, die Ruten Gold und Regen,
der Weißdorn im Geröll: Kein Ziel steht mehr entgegen.

Oktoberkälte

Zu spät? Schon längst verloren? Die Fliege glaubt es nicht.
Sie kriecht noch immer weiter und weiter hin zum Licht.

The crossing

The same old path, the canes of gold and rain,
the hawthorn in the stony field: no goal standing in its way.

October cold snap

Too late? Too mislaid? Not according to the fly,
skittering ever deeper into the light.

Zwei Äpfel
Vierter November 2016, Breitenau

Pupillenrund und rot, der Apfel lockt von weit.
So heißt der kahle Baum: Durchbrochen liegt die Zeit.

Zwölfter November 2016, Goldpomäne am Haus

Ein Schattenwirren, süß verströmt das Jahr im Mund.
So heißt der erste Biß: Gedächtnis ohne Grund.

Two apples
November fourth 2016, Breitenau

The apple beckons from afar, its pupil red and round.
Thus the name of the barren tree: time broken down.

November twelfth 2016, golden russets by the house

In the stir of shadows, time melts sweetly in the mouth.
Thus the name of the first bite: memory without ground.

from WINDSTROKES
(2015)

Breitenau (Osterzgebirge)

«Tröste dich! Du würdest mich nicht suchen,
wenn du mich nicht gefunden hättest.»
—Pascal

Wo ich herkam, weiß ich nicht sicher zu sagen. Die Wege
tragen keine Namen. Die Häuser, wohin sie mich führen
über Reste von Schneefeldern, stehen wie Falken im Ostwind.
Nebel aus dem böhmmiischen Becken geboren, im Reifglanz,
letztes Dorf vor der Grenze, die Felsen sinken wie schlafend,
breitstirnig, kalt, sie tranken aus der sächsischen Lethe.
Eingedunkelt die Augen, Schläfen wie weiß überschimmelt:
Das ich mich erinnere, wer mag das behaupten?
Eulen hausen im Kirchturm, sie hocken sich nachts auf die Zeiger:
So wird es später hell, erwachen zögernd die Ginster,
wippen im Harsch. Der Hund fällt zurück, ein beharrliches Echo
geht über Moos, Geröll, das dumpf und beständig sich gleich bleibt.
Gestern noch wußte ich, woran ich glaubte—an die Gebilde
warmer Lippen, Hauch und Laut; und die letzten Gehöfte
unter dem Sattel öffnen die Tore: So laß ich mich trieben,
hier und da noch ein Fetzen Landschaft, ein schlappendes Windrad.
Was ich vergaß, das findet mich wieder, wie eine Spiegelung,
klarer jedoch und gehüllt in ein milderes Licht von den Bergen.

Breitenau (Eastern Ore Mountains)

> "Take comfort! You would not seek me had
> you not found me."
>
> —Pascal

Where I came from, I cannot say for sure. These paths
bear no names. The houses to which they lead
over the remains of snowfields hover in the east wind like hawks.
Fog born from the Bohemian basin, and aglow in the distance,
the last village before the border, the rocks sinking into sleep,
broad-browed, cold, having drunk from Saxony's Lethe.
The eyes dim, the temples mildewed with white:
That it is me who remembers, who could make this claim?
Owls housed in the church steeple, crouched on the clock hands at night:
Then daybreak, the broom plants struggling awake, whipped
this way and that in the crusted snow. The dogs fall back, an echo
drifts across the moss in a long and muffled likeness of itself.
Just yesterday I still knew what it was I believed in—the shape
of warm lips, breath, and musical tones; and the last few farmyards
below the Saddle open their gates: I let myself be borne along,
here and there another patch of landscape, a windmill's clatter.
What I forgot now finds me again, like a mirror image,
though far clearer, framed by this mild mountain light.

Aquarium

Frei sein? Schal erscheint's bei den Spielglungen, Schönheit der Wesen
hinter Glas in der Strömung, die ich versunken verfolge:
Kreise der Haie, Bahnen des Mondfischs und fliegende Rochen,
stark with Gezeiten... Und sehe ich später zerbissene Flossen,
weiße, flockige Wunden, so tilgt sie ein matteres Leuchten,
überblendet die Leiber, treibt sie, betäubt, ins Vergessen...
Dort also sitze ich, wirke gewiß, bin bar aller Obhut,
Fische umkreisen mich, schnappen mein Augenlicht auf und
    verschwinden.
Rote Medusen fasern ins Wasser, in pulsender Stille
schweben Gewölbe, fliehen, wie flüssiges Glas ihre Körper,
fein geblasen ins Nichts—diese Schleier, sind sie nicht zeitlos?

    Ein Solitär und Segler, große Qualle,
    die Nesselfäden lang, in Majestät
    die hohle Form, um Kraft zu fassen:
    Beständigkeit gibt ihr ein Widerhallen,
    ein immer Gleiches, nie zu spät
    und nie zu früh, sich zu verlassen
    auf Seegang, den sie in sich spürt,
    der sie auf engstem Raum ins Weite führt.

Aquarium

To be free? An empty question, it would seem, as I follow these creatures
in all their sunken streaming mirrored beauty behind the glass:
the sharks as they circle, the moonfish as they wax and wane, the rays
in flight, as telling as the tides... followed by the sight of chewed-up fins,
white wounded blurs of skin, with the light now growing far more matte,
the bodies caught in a slow dissolve, numbed into oblivion...
And I here I sit on my own, reflecting on this, encircled by fish
that snap at the light in my eye, then disappear from sight.
Red jellyfish fray in the water, pulse in the stillness, domes
afloat, in flight, their bodies like liquid glass finely blown
into the void, veils of timelessness.

A solitary seafarer, the medusa,
majestic in her many-fringed train,
a cup in which to capture power,
persists, an echo of herself,
forever the same, never too early
or too late to venture out to sea
as she journeys in, every contraction
widening her sphere of action.

Wer beharrte, gestoßen in Träume, auf äußeren Grenzen?
Bilder, mit nichts zu vergleichen, entbunden von Sinn und von
     Schwerkraft:
Sonnenstern, Mönchsfisch, Seepferdchen, Dornhecht und schwarze
     Muräne...
absolute Partikel, Monaden, fraglos vorhanden,
ohne Grund und Ziel im blauen, sich krümmenden Kosmos.
Seetulpin meditieren auf Schläuchen das Meer in den Becken:

    «Gegrüßet seiest Du: Rauschen. Nichts,
    was ich bin—Du in mir, geschaut
    durch meinen Mund, geatmet und verdaut.
    Hast Du ein Ufer? In mir? Als Verzicht?
    Du strömst durch mich, und ich bin Haut,
    Gefäß, Dein stummes Gleichgewicht?»

Lippen am Glas, als küßten Mensch und Fisch einen Spiegel—
innen friert es wohl, doch erwidern kann niemand das Glänzen.
Hier, ein Bretrachter, und dort der Thun, dessen Augen mich meidet:
Schlafende, von der Natur im Stich gelassene Körper?
Namen auf Tafeln, und wie kein Benennen sei ohne Sehnsucht,
fallen die Blick jäh ins Offene starrer Pupillen.

Who were they, plunged into dream, nudging the glass?
Images, comparable to nothing, free from gravity or signification,
sunstar, monkfish, seahorse, dogfish, black moray eel...
absolute particles, monads, their evidence beyond question,
without ground, without aim, in this cosmos doubled-up in blue.
Their bulbs abob in the tank, the sea tulips imagine oceans:

> "Welcome, Power of Sound! I'm nothing
> alike—You in me, glimpsed
> through my mouth, breathed in, broken down.
> Where's your shore? In me? Your inner maze?
> You flow through me, am I your skin,
> your vessel, your mute counterweight?"

Lips to the pane, as if man and fish were kissing a looking glass.
But it's cold inside, the brightness meets with no reply.
Here an observer, there a tuna refusing to meet my eye:
These sleeping bodies, left by Nature to their own devices?
Names on panels, but as no naming can occur without desire,
every gaze gets lost in this open reach of blank stares.

Die Libelle

Sie ist mir eingegeben, die Libelle,
ein stilles Komma in der Luft, sie steht,
als ihr das Graslicht in die Augen weht,
noch immer zögert sie an einer Stelle...

Weil die Bewegungen nicht ihre waren?
Weil nichts erklärt, wie etwas folgen soll?
Weil das, was kommt, nicht uns gehört, und voll
die Flügel stehen, voll von Unsichtbarem?

Und wie sie zittert, ist sie ganz für sich—
ein unwägbares, schwebendes Gestein.
Ein blaues Licht schließt sie von innen ein.

Ich sehe ihren Glanz—er schaut doch mich.
Wie aufgereihte Perlen, ihre Glieder,
in ihrem Schimmer kehrt der Sommer wieder.

Dragonfly

This dragonfly supplies me a key,
a standstill comma in the sky,
grasslight streaming to her eye,
hesitating where or what to be.

Because such encounters, not of her making?
Because nothing explains what might follow?
Because our futures are so hollow?
Our wings so full, our eyes mistaken?

How she thrums, all out for herself,
A gem punching above her weight,
Blue light nailing her into place.

I see what she's looking at: myself.
Her limbs, pearls on strings,
In her shimmer, summer again begins.

Der Gott, den es nicht gibt, in mir ein dunkler Riß
Ist meiner Seele nah, so oft ich ihn vermiß.

The god, who doesn't exist, in me a dark rift,
So near to my soul, whenever it's him I miss.

archipelago books

is a non-profit publisher devoted to
promoting cross-cultural exchange through innovative
classic and contemporary international literature
archipelagobooks.org

elsewhere editions

translates luminous picture books from around the world
elsewhereeditions.org